God's World

Poetry
for
Reflection

Sandy Bohon LMHC

Dedication

This book is dedicated to my father
Glenn R. Bohon,
and his deep love for poetry.

Drizzling Rain

Drizzle, Drizzle goes the rain
As it hits my window pane.
Many thoughts are on my mind,
Some I should leave behind...
Many things I need to do,
Or maybe it's just a few.
But tomorrow is another day,
So, I think I'll sit and pray,
And I will dream and ponder,
Let my mind go 'round and yonder,
And enjoy the drizzling rain,
That softly hits my window pane.

Facing Reality

To look into our life
    And face reality,
We cannot look to hard,
    For fear of what we'll see.

We need to coat our vision,
    With a plan and dream,
And being optimistic
    Easier life will seem.

"May these words of my mouth and
this meditation of my heart be pleasing
in Your sight, Lord, my Rock and my
Redeemer." (Psalm 19:14)

Double Vision

Along this life we travel through
Light and dark are all around,
Evil wants to ensnare you
Beating a deafening sound.

Through foggy mist we can't see
All the good that blends with sin,
Mixing dark with reality,
We call this double vision.

Through the mist we see a light
It is Jesus shining in,
Only He can restore your sight
And give you single vision.

Serving Christ

Whatever life may bring my way,
   My hopes and dreams
   Or evil things,
I hope that I can always say,
   I trusted You
   To see me through.

But it things do not go right,
   To not give in
   And not to sin,
I hope I can stand up and fight,
   For victory win
   For I serve Him.

And if things are going well,
   For me to see
   That Christ helps me,
And that I may always tell,
   That God above
   Sends me His love.

"Neither do people light a lamp and put it under a bowl.
Instead they put it on its stand, and it gives light to
everyone in the house. In the same way, let your light
shine before others, that they may see your good deeds
and glorify your Father in heaven." (Matthew 5:15,16)

My Life's a Mess

When trouble comes into my life
   I'm shaking like a tree
All my leaves fall to the ground
   And my branch is bare to see.

My neighbor came along and said,
   "Your leaves are on the ground!"
All I could do was whisper
   "My faith cannot be found."

My friend said, "Your life's a mess
   That's not what the Bible teaches,
You are to study the Word
   And put your faith in Jesus."

So, I listened to my neighbor
   And put my faith in Jesus
Because He is our foundation
   And He will never leave us.

Help Me be a Blessing

Lord, help me be a blessing
　To someone today,
These thoughts I'm expressing
　And this I will pray.

Lord, help me look at others
　And see the good inside,
Because we all are brothers
　And for each of us You died.

Lord, help me think of You
　Because of all You've done for me
And all You've seen me through
　From now till eternity.

"Do not be anxious about anything, but in every situation, by prayer and petition, with thanksgiving, present your requests to God. And the peace of God, which transcends all understanding, will guard your hearts and minds in Christ Jesus." (Philippians 4:6,7)

Floating Memories

A raindrop falls and disappears
And blends in with the pond,
Dreams are swirling in my mind
Here and there and far beyond.

One day you're here, and then you're gone
All I have left are memories
Of things we did, places seen
Softly floating in the breeze.

Wandering Heart

My heart is like a wandering star
   Passing through the night
Reaching out to others
   In my lonely flight.

Sometimes my heart will rest
   On someone in the way
Who doesn't feel it's touch,
   Or want my heart to stay.

So off again to wander
   In the stillness of the night
Reaching out to others
   In my lonely plight.

"The Lord is close to the brokenhearted
and saves those who are crushed in
spirit." (Psalm 34:18)

God Made Me

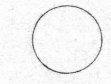

The oceans, rivers, and lakes,
   The mountains and trees I see,
Were created by the hand of God
   Not by the will of me.

Birds flying high and lions roar,
   Wild horses on ranges run free,
Were created by the hand of God
   Not by the will of me.

Before creation of the earth
   Christ in His foreknowledge could see
That in a certain point in time
   He'd make a person as me.

"You alone are the Lord. You made the heavens, even the highest heavens, and all their starry host, the earth and all that is on it, the seas and all that is in them. You give life to everything, and the multitudes of heaven worship you." (Nehemiah 9:6)

God's Blessings

The closer I've drawn to God
The more I'm able to see,
That God is a God of love
With blessings in store for me.

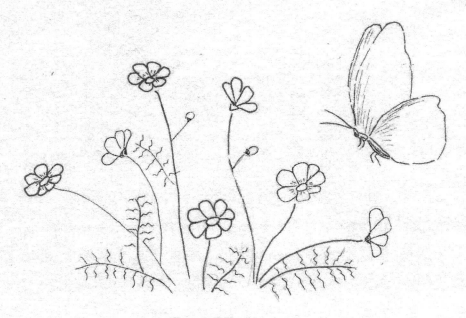

Love is Like a Butterfly

Love is like a butterfly,
   Lighting here and there,
Very fickle in its flight
   With its love to share.

And like the butterfly,
   Lights many times a day,
In our lives, love touches us
   In many different ways.

So, do not be illusioned,
   Thinking love is what you're in,
'Cause tomorrow might bring another
   And your love will start again.

So, trust in God to help you see
   The one He has for you,
Where your souls can be one
   In a love that will be true.

The Word Love

To some people love is just a word,
   That's easy for them to say,
Because it doesn't mean much to them
   They use it to get their way.

Others never say it at all,
   Because to them, it's understood,
And we know this is also wrong
   To speak it often they should.

To me, love is not just a word
   But of feelings from the soul,
And to those who give and receive it
   It makes their being whole.

And even thought I've told you
   In many different ways,
I'll love you with all my heart
   All my life long days.

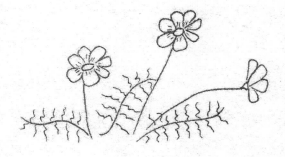

"Trust in the Lord with all your heart and lean
not on your own understanding; in all your ways
submit to Him, and He will make your paths
straight." (Proverbs 3:5,6)

What Could Have Been

What could have been, I'll never know
What was, will always be
Life's not fair I tell myself
To live in my - reality.

I live my life, past is past
The future also seems dark,
To have never been with you
To have never shared my heart.

So, I will sit and ponder life
And wish things ought to be,
And soon I'll drop off to sleep
To end my misery.

But in my dreams, you are there
As elusive as a thought,
When I awake you are gone,
But a glimpse of you I caught.

What Ifs

I think about my life today,
    And I think about the past
Thinking about the good times
    Memories that always last.

But sometimes I want to change
    Things I did back then,
I wish I'd taken different paths
    And different thoughts within.

'What ifs' go through my mind
    And different paths I'd take,
Would I be happier now
    With changes I would make?

Maybe the paths I've taken
    Are the correct ones for me
Lord, help me accept my life
    And set my memories free.

"The Lord is my Shepherd, I lack nothing. He makes me lie down in green pastures, He leads me beside quiet waters, He refreshes my soul. He guides me along the right paths for His name's sake." (Psalm 23:1-3)

My Redeemer

My Redeemer came to earth
  To shed His blood for me,
Though I'm the one who sinned
  On the cross, He died for me.

And Satan could not stop,
  No matter how he tried,
Christ hung upon that cross
  For me that day, He died.

If I lose my life on earth
  My treasures in heaven I place,
My life will not be in vain
  When I see Him face to face.

Help Me Tell Others

So busy I get in my life
There's so many things to do
That I sometimes forget, Lord
To be telling others of you.

I know that you died for my sin
And I'll be in heaven one day
But please don't let me forget
To help show others the way.

For heaven and hell's forever
And life on this earth is fleeting
Help me to have a deep burden
That others to heaven I'll bring.

"How, then, can they call on the one they have not believed in? And how can they believe in the one of whom they have not heard? And how can they hear without someone preaching to them? And how can they preach unless they are sent? As it is written, 'How beautiful are the feet of those who bring good news!'" (Romans 10:14,15)

My Friend Amy

I have a friend who is very dear,
    And Amy is her name,
Why we're friends is very clear
    But our habits aren't the same.

Amy's home is always spotless
    She cleans it every day,
My home is such a mess,
    I don't know what to say.

Amy loves helping others,
    She has a heart of gold,
She gives advice to young mothers,
    Their children she helps mold.

Every one should have a friend
    As faithful as my Amy,
Whose cuts and sores she will mend
    And treat you as her family.

"This is how we know what love is: Jesus Christ
laid down His life for us. And we ought to lay down
our lives for our brothers and sisters. If anyone has
material possessions and sees a brother or sister
in need but has no pity on them, how can the love
of God be in that person? Dear children, let us not
love with words or speech but with actions and in
truth." (1 John 3:16-18)

Annette

Let me tell you about my friend
  She's as crazy as can be,
She exercises every day
  And runs circles around me.

Annette gobbles down her food
  But is skinny as a rail,
She likes her coffee very dark
  While mine is somewhat pale.

Annette is very animated
  And flails her arms when talking,
She's so funny we laugh and laugh
  While 'round the room she's squawking.

Though we are very different
  Which is very plain to see,
Everyone needs a friend like mine,
  Who's as special as can be.

Thank You, Lord

Did I thank you Lord today
For the blessings you give me?
   For the birds that sing
   The flowers in spring
And the mountains that I see.

Did I thank you Lord today
For the love you've shown my way?
   For my husband near
   My children dear
And the love we share each day.

But most of all I thank you Lord
For Christ that you did give
   For my sins to pay
   On the cross that day,
Eternal life in heaven to live.

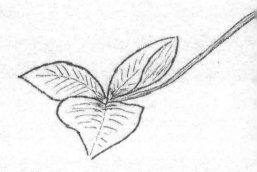

"The Spirit Himself testifies with our spirit that we are God's children. Now if we are children, then we are heirs - heirs of God and co-heirs with Christ, if indeed we share in His sufferings in order that we may also share in His glory." (Romans 8:16,17)

Joint-Heirs with Christ

Though I am but flesh and blood
My life a passing flower,
In eternal time this life is brief
Like a summer shower.

And though I was but nothing
Upon Christ's payment I did believe,
Now I've become joint-heirs with Christ
Eternal life in heaven to receive.

Fruit of the Spirit

Love your neighbors as yourself
    As the Scriptures write,
Joy will come into your life
    You'll be a shining light.

Peace will come and calm your soul
    As only Christ can give,
Patience keeps your eyes on God
    As to others we forgive.

Kindness brings our friends together
    To live in harmony,
Goodness is a solid rock
    That keeps our family free.

Faithfulness is a tie that binds
    Our unity in the Spirit
As we live our lives for Jesus
    We'll have fruit of the Spirit.

But the Fruit of
the Spirit is love, joy,
peace, patience, kindness,
goodness, faithfulness,
gentleness, self-control;
against such things
there is no law.

Galatians 5:22,23

Give Thoughts to God

Lord, it's with a heavy heart,
    I come to you today,
Many thoughts are on my mind
    I don't know what to say.

My friends have heavy burdens
    And with them I try to share,
It all seems overwhelming
    To reach each one with care.

They don't reach out to You,
    Or want You in their life
No matter what I say to them
    They continue with their strife.

So, I come before You, Lord,
    The true helper of mankind
I give all my thoughts to You,
    In You true peace we find.

"Even youths grow tired and weary, and young men stumble and fall; but those who hope in the Lord will renew their strength. They will soar on wings like eagles; they will run and not grow weary, they will walk and not be faint." (Isaiah 40:30,31)

Jesus My Sustainer

Trials and troubles are everywhere
   Discouragements are all around
While reaching out to others
   Not a friend could be found.

Darkness swirls around me
   And in its depths, I fall
Sorrow fills my heart -
   Then to Jesus, I call.

Jesus says, "Come to Me,"
   His friendship can be found
He's the sustainer of my life,
   His love and care abound.

Life life Now

Memories from the past
    keep coming to my mind
Should I ponder on these,
    or keep them far behind.
Some memories are pleasant,
    others are not so
Should I dwell on them,
    or let them slowly go.
Thinking about things
    in the near future,
Do I want them,
    I'm not so sure,
But I'm in the present
    now in my life,
The future and past
    are causing me strife.
Why can't I just enjoy
    the present - now.
So, I'll pray to God
    that He'll show me how,
And He'll give me wisdom
    to help me to see,
To live my life now,
    where I ought to be.

"Brothers and sisters, I do not consider myself yet to have taken hold of it. But one thing I do: Forgetting what is behind and straining toward what is ahead, I press on toward the goal to win the prize for which God has called me heavenward in Christ Jesus." (Philippians 3:13,14)

Keep Eyes on Jesus

Sometimes I get discouraged
When troubles come my way
I get my eyes off Jesus,
Feelings take over my day.

When my eyes are on me
And the problems that I face
Then gloom overcomes me,
And my joy it will erase.

But when I put my focus
Again, on Jesus above
He'll help me with my troubles
And keep me in His love.

Life's Unfair

Falling, Falling,
Into despair,
Scratching, scratching,
Into the air,
Bending, turning,
Into nowhere,
Calling, crying,
Life's unfair.

Then a voice said to all,
"Life is what you make it,"
Take control of yourself,
And don't give in and quit.

Because life is a journey
A path we all must take,
Let the Lord help you
In the choices that you make.

Do not give up to crying
Stand tall on your two feet,
With the help of Jesus
The unfairness can be beat.

"Have I not commanded you? Be strong and
courageous. Do not be afraid; do not be
discouraged, for the Lord your God will be with
you wherever you go." (Joshua 1:9)

Christ Gives Peace

My friend has many problems
    Her life stays in a mess
She is forever overwhelmed
    Her life is full of stress.

She calls and talks to me
    And I try to help her out
When I talk about God's love
    She complains about self doubt.

She doesn't believe in Jesus
    Who paid for all her sin
Only He can give her peace
    And help her soul within.

So, I'll continue to pray
    That my friend one day will know
That Christ can give her peace
    And His love to her will show.

P E A C E

Let My Light Shine

Lord give me the love to see
That we're all sinners saved by grace,
That someday in heaven we'll be
Where we'll see You face to face.

Lord give me the courage to tell
Others about how You died,
On the cross to save us from hell,
So in heaven they can abide.

Lord give me the wisdom to live
A holy life for You each day,
So to others, I can give
A light to show them the way.

"For you were once darkness, but now you are light in
the Lord. Live as children of light (for the fruit of the
light consists in all goodness, righteousness and truth)
and find out what pleases the Lord." (Ephesians 5:8-10)

Children of Light

There is a gulf between darkness and light,
Between Satan and following the Lord,
There is a ship that sets out to sea,
That all Christians should be aboard.

The earth left behind is the darkness,
The ship out to sea is the light,
The earth is the world and its pleasures,
Where Satan, his demons do fight.

We shouldn't live our lives in the world,
For in Christ we are children of light,
By leaving the world in darkness behind,
We live in the ship of God's might.

God Wants Me

I have not much to offer
Life's not been good to me,
I have not fame and fortune
In fact, I'm poor, you see.

I saw life passing me by
My youth I cannot regain,
Each day was like the other
Every face I met the same.

Christ came and spoke to me
He wiped my tears with His hand,
"I've chosen you to follow me
Out of thousands in the land."

I gave my life to the Lord
Because He wants all of me,
He'll use me for His purpose
Whatever that may be.

"And we know that in all things God works for the good of those who love Him, who have been called according to His purpose." (Romans 8:28)

Trusting God

Lord, why do I have trouble
   Trusting You each day,
Why do I have this doubting
   Not listening to what You say?

I know You'll take care of me
   But my heart doesn't agree,
So I'm stuck in the middle
   Living in misery.

But the Lord said to me,
   Trust Me with all your heart
And when you truly do,
   All your fears will depart.

The Lord knows what's best for me
   And in His time I'll know
That everything will turn out right,
   Blessings from Him will flow.

God Made the Moon Above

God made the moon above,
  And the stars to shine at night,
By day He made the sun to rise,
  To give us heat and light.

God made the rain to fall,
  To water the plants and trees,
God made the cats and dogs,
  And butterflies, birds, and bees.

Everything you see was made,
  By God up high above,
And He wants you to know
  He also sends His love.

Each New Day

As flowers bloom in the spring
And leaves change in the fall
Each new day God will bring
Blessings for each and all.

"Lift up your eyes and look to the heavens: Who created all these? He who brings out the starry host one by one and calls forth each of them by name. Because of His great power and mighty strength, not one of them is missing." (Isaiah 40:26)

Tapping Rain

The beating rain is on my roof
   Drowning out the sound,
Of a heart that has been broken
   Of a love that wasn't found.

All the miles between us
   And the time between each call
Hasn't decreased my feelings
   And to my knees I fall.

I pray to God to take away
   This never-ending pain
So I can listen to the quiet,
   Of the tapping of the rain.

Broken Heart

Among the remains
 Of my broken heart,
Is the beginning
 Of a new start.

"Wait for the Lord; be strong and take heart
and wait for the Lord." (Psalm 27:14)

Yearning Inside

God tells me to be patient
    But how long must I wait
This yearning I have inside
    Wanting to know my fate.

The door that doesn't knock
    The phone that never rings
My heart is being broken
    With love that never brings.

God tells me to trust Him,
    I know that is the way,
So, I must try harder,
    And to Jesus I will pray.

"Forget the former things; do not dwell on the past.
See, I am doing a new thing! Now it springs up; do
you not perceive it? I am making a way in the wilder-
ness and streams in the wasteland." (Isaiah 43:18,19)

All Alone

On Valentine's Day I'm all alone
    Another year passes by,
As others give gifts and celebrate
    I look at my cat and sigh.

But being along is OK
    When thinking about the choices,
I'd rather be by myself
    Then arguing and loud voices.

So, I will just be content
    Until God will bring my way
A nice person whom He will chose,
    Till then, single I'll stay.

God's Timing

There is a man I want so much
His eyes to see, his hands to touch
His warm embrace I want to feel
Our lives together I want to seal
Our children freely in love to hold
Our thoughts and dreams together mold.

I want him now but I can wait
To have him mine, in some future date
For the times not right, this I know
For my deep love for him to show
So I will wait and abide the time
Until I can say, he now is mine.

You wonder why I want this man?
Our future together I will plan!
His eyes are kind his love I feel
His arms are strong his values real
His mind is sound, his love flows free,
Himself to give, I know he'll be.

So unto God each day I pray
For I do know He'll find a way
When timings right God will bring
Us together with His blessing
So, I'll not worry for God will see,
That one day he will be with me.

"Love is patient, love is kind. It does not envy, it does
not boast, it is not proud. It does not dishonor others,
it is not self-seeking, it is not easily angered, it keeps
no record of wrongs. Love does not delight in evil but
rejoices with the truth. It always protects, always trusts,
always hopes, always perseveres." (1 Corinthians 13,4-7)

Poem to My Love

The rose of all the flowers
  Is the symbol of true love,
And peace is a pure and clear
  As the whiteness of a dove.

Poetry is my deepest thoughts
  That lies within my soul,
And expressing them to you
  It makes my being whole.

And I wanted you to know
  That all the things above,
Is how I feel since we met,
  And with you I fell in love.

Morning Breeze

As the morning rays peep out
Amongst the background of the trees,
Birds are chirping out their song
Hidden among the leaves.
God is Lord of all the earth
From the mountains to the seas,
Sending out His love to all
In the gentleness of the breeze.

God's Provisions

Some people live their lives believing
Whatever they have they earned,
The harder they work, the more they have
Whatever is given out is returned.

But they are forgetting one great fact,
That everything comes from above,
God gives us health and food on our table,
And showers us with His love.

"He who forms the mountains, who creates the wind,
who reveals His thoughts to mankind, who turns dawn
to darkness, and treads on the heights of the earth -
the Lord God Almighty is His name." (Amos 4:13

Negative People

Many people are negative
Their thoughts are dark and gloom,
There is no joy in their life
Like dead bodies in a tomb.

They spread their negative thoughts
On everyone they're around
Like poison in a serpent
Their evil does abound.

But they'll have a day of judgment,
And Karma can be cruel.
So, don't be a negative person
And live by the golden rule.

"As a prisoner for the Lord, then, I urge you to live a life worthy of the calling you have received. Be completely humble and gentle; be patient, bearing with one another in love." (Ephesians 4:1,2)

Patience

P raying
A lways
T o
I gnore
E verything
N egative
C oncerning
E veryone.

The Ungodly

The ungodly the Bible says
Are as dark clouds without rain
Autumn trees without fruit
Distributing their pain.

They are wild waves upon the sea
Casting around their shame
Wandering stars in darkness
Using others for their gain.

The ungodly are mockers
Causing divisions and much strife
Like unreasoning animals
Destroying their own life.

So, do not be ungodly,
Keep yourself in God's love
As He sends down His mercy
And blessings from above.

"These people are blemishes at your love feasts, eating with you without the slightest qualm - shepherds who feed only themselves. They are clouds without rain, blown along by the wind: autumn trees, without fruit and uprooted - twice dead. They are wild waves of the sea, foaming up their shame; wandering stars, for whom blackest darkness has been reserved forever.

But you, dear friends, by building yourselves up in your most holy faith and praying in the Holy Spirit, keep yourselves in God's love as you wait for the mercy of our Lord Jesus Christ to bring you to eternal life." (Jude 12,13,20,21)

The Wicked

The path of the wicked is darkness
They can't sleep till evil is done,
They eat the bread of wickedness
Out of their mouth violence doth run.

The wicked do not seek the Lord
They say 'there's no God' in their heart,
While spewing out deceit, and discord,
God's goodness and values, they depart.

But the wicked do not realize
That there will come a judgment day
They will stand before the Lord with cries
As in the graves their bodies lay.

Wishes

I wish I was a millionaire,
   With a Rolls Royce at my door,
Then I could ride in style
   From the mountains to the shore.

I wish I had a long fur coat
   To wear when it is cold,
And five walk-in closets
   For all my clothes to hold.

I wish I had three children
   Who never ever fought,
Who always did what was told
   And never a cold was caught.

But wishes are like dreams,
   And in the morning fade away,
So, what I wish the most for
   Is to accept my life each day.

"Trust in the Lord and do good; dwell in the land and enjoy safe pasture. Take delight in the Lord, and He will give you the desires of your heart."
(Psalm 37:3,4)

My Dreams

As the leaf passes by in the streams
So my thoughts reflect on my dreams,
    The reality of what will be
    Or the affect it has on me,
The blending of both it seems,
Allow me to continue my dreams.

The Night Snow

Snow is falling softly down
    Making nature pure white,
Over in the distant town
    There comes a glowing light.

Through the darkness comes around,
    The moon shines forth its light,
The beauties of God still abound
    In the quietness of the night.

"You alone are the Lord. You made the heavens, even the highest heavens, and all their starry host, the earth and all that is on it, the seas and all that is in them. You give life to everything, and the multitudes of heaven worship You." (Nehemiah 9:6)

Christmas Tree

Christmas tree
All shimmering bright,
Lights sparkling
Into the night.
Memories past
Filtering out,
Thoughts anew
Drifting about.
Thoughts anew
Drifting about.

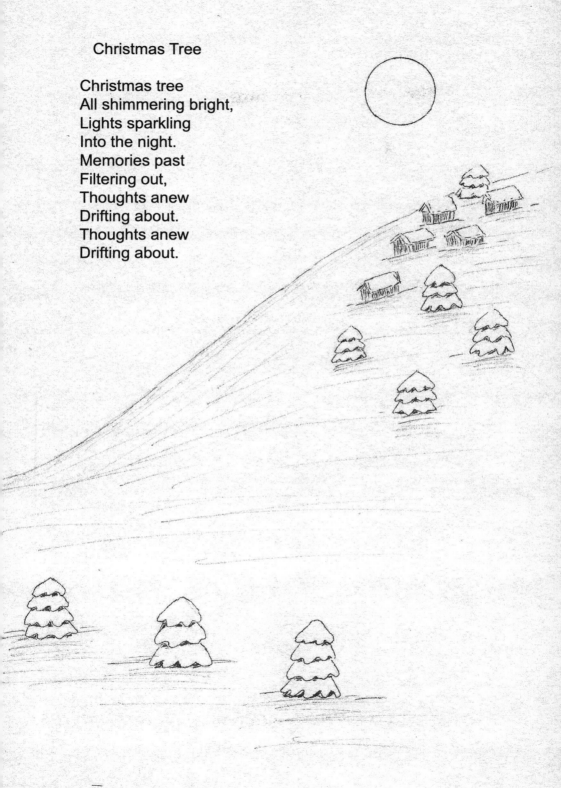

Thinking of You

Thinking of you brings memories back
The good times we felt and shared,
Walks in the snow with cold on our face
And over the streams we dared.

Thinking of you brings the future near
And together again we'll be,
Snowing outside with the fireplace glowing,
Reflections in our heart we'll see.

Thoughts of You

Even though we're miles apart
I feel your presence near,
   Your tone of voice
   The things you said
Speaks softly in my ear.

Soon we'll be together
Never again to part,
   The love you showed
   When you were here
Is felt within my heart.

"May the Lord keep watch between you and me when
we are away from each other." (Genesis 31:49b)

Starting Over

While we're passing through this life
   We make friends along the way,
We have our jobs and families
   To take up all our day.

One by one our friends are gone,
   And our lives are broken up,
Our jobs have changed and we move on
   By ourselves each night we sup.

Then we sit and realize
   It's a crossroad that we've found,
That the past is left behind
   No ties to us are bound.

The future again looks bright
   On the new road we will find,
New friends and new commitments
   As those we left behind.

Being Alone

My life has changed, my friends are gone
   And I am left alone
Is it fair I ask myself that,
   Into this life I'm thrown.

But being alone has brought me back
   To God who's willing to hear,
And I will never be alone again
   For God is always near.

"He guides the humble in what is right and teaches them
His way. All the ways of the Lord are loving and faithful."
(Psalm 25:9,10a)

Christian's Purpose

When we trust Christ as our Savior
We don't die and go to heaven,
God wants us on this earth
There's a purpose we have from Him.

God wants Christians to love Him
And follow Him in every way,
This means to live holy lives
And put God first in our day.

God wants us to tell others
That Christ died upon the cross,
That He freely gave His life
And shed His blood for us.

"Don't you have a saying, 'It's still four months until harvest'? I tell you, open your eyes and look at the fields! They are ripe for harvest." (John 4:35)

Treasures in Heaven

My body grows old and weary,
My life on this earth is through,
Looking back I'd change nothing
For a secret in life, I knew.

Riches and power are fleeting
At the grave they are left behind,
If you live your life for Christ,
Then treasures in heaven you'll find.

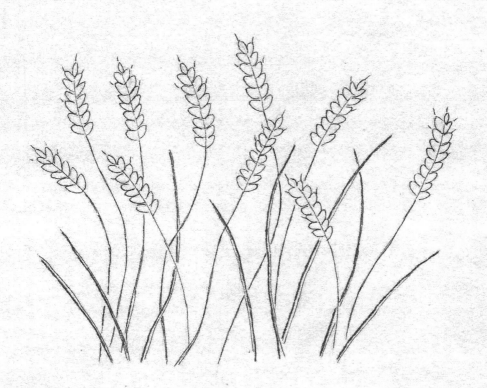

Feeling Sad

I woke up sad today,
    I didn't know why,
My heart was so heavy,
    Life passing me by.

I get into these moods
    Feeling sad, anxiety
Of regrets from the past,
    What the future will bring.

Then I thought of Jesus
    And all He's done for me,
He tells us to be content
    And live worry free.

If we are praising Jesus,
    Filing our heart with song
There's no room for sadness,
    Praising Him all day long.

"Rejoice in the Lord always. I will say it again;
Rejoice!" (Philippians 4:4)

"Rejoice always, pray continually, give thanks
in all circumstances; for this is God's will for you
in Christ Jesus." (1 Thessalonians 5:16-18)

My Prayers

My prayers seem unanswered
   Going up, back to the floor,
Like a distant unheard word
   Floating around to never more.

Why do my thoughts contradict -
   The Bible says God hears me,
Are my thoughts in conflict -
   Not based on reality?

The Bible says God loves me
   And that He very much cares,
That He smiles down upon me
   And listens to my prayers.

So, I need to trust in Jesus
   Filling my heart with song,
And not make up excuses,
   Praying all the day long.

Pray without ceasing

Delusions

What could have been
Will never be
Open my eyes,
And help me see.
    Illusions -
    Delusions -
Are swirling around.

    My life is a haze,
    Like mice in a maze,
Deceptions abound -

Spiraling down
    Into the hole
I reached to God
    To save my soul.

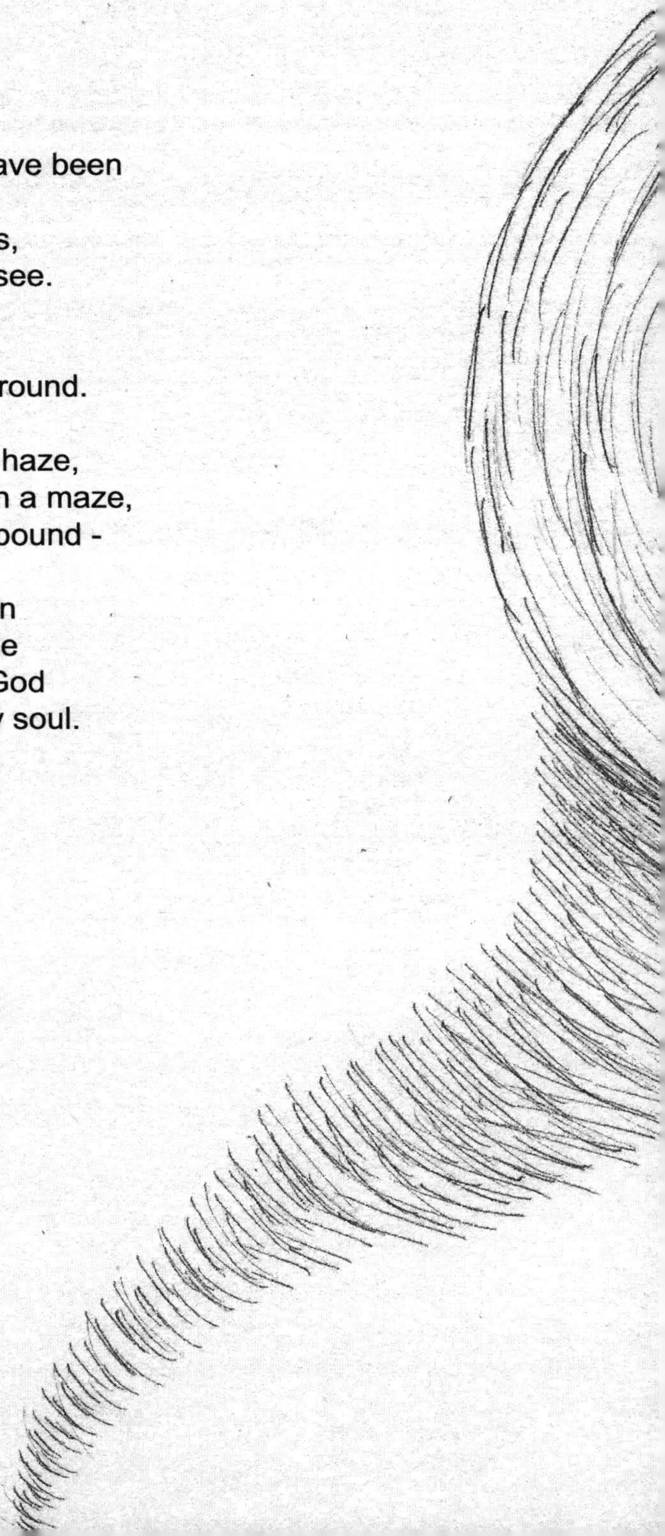

"So do not fear, for I am with you; do not be dismayed, for I am your God. I will strengthen you and help you; I will uphold you with my righteous right hand." (Isaiah 41:10)

Regrets

There's regrets I have in the past
   If I stop and upon them dwell,
There are also many great things
   That have turned out quite well.

So, I'll let the unpleasant
   Be overcome by things of good,
And be content with where I am
   And not regret, I should.

Far as the east is to the west,
   That's where God has put my sin,
No longer shall I wrest,
   My joy is now to begin.

"For as high as the heavens are above the earth, so great is His love for those who fear Him: as far as the east is from the west, so far has He removed our transgressions from us." (Psalm 103:11,12)

God's Christian

Lord, I look back on my day
And know I've failed again,
I always try to be so good
But something comes up, and then...

And so, I pray again tonight
To help me tomorrow to be,
The kind of Christian that You want,
And the type that I want to be.

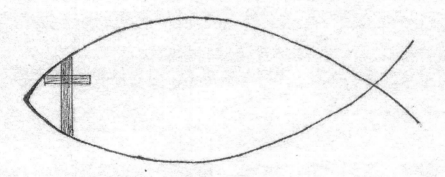

God is Love

Keep Your Morals Strong

In this world we live on
Where right has turned to wrong
We need to keep our character
And our morals strong.

With Satan and his lure
He makes us feel unsure
But the Holy Spirit inside
Will make our conscience stir.

If in Christ we will abide,
He will help us to ride
And keep our heads above
The worlds deep sinful tide.

With pureness of a dove
With much help from above
Abiding in God's love
We can keep our morals strong.

"Praise be to the God and Father of our Lord Jesus
Christ, who has blessed us in the heavenly realms
with every spiritual blessing in Christ." (Ephesians 1:3)

Trust in the Lord

Trust in the Lord the Bible says
    And in Him be content -
But why is it so difficult
    And why my soul I wrent?

God created the heavens and earth
    He also created me,
Just listen to what the Bible says,
    And let God's love flow free.

Trust in Him with all your heart
    And don't let doubt creep in,
Rest in His amazing grace
    And He'll bless your soul within.

"I pray that out of His glorious riches He may strengthen
you with power through His Spirit in your inner being, so
that Christ may dwell in your hearts through faith. And
I pray that you, being rooted and established in love, may
have power, together with all the Lord's holy people, to
grasp how wide and long and high and deep is the love
of Christ." (Ephesians 3:16-18)

Key to Happiness

I wanted fame and fortune
Instead, I was cold and poor,
I wanted love and happiness
To enter into my door.

But the knock that came was Christ
His entering in I did find,
He's the key to happiness
And my mind before was blind.

God's Will Now

I feel I want to move on
But I don't know where to go,
I wish God would speak to me
His will for me He'd show.

But God did speak to me,
"You're in My will now," said He.

"And when the time is ready
The door will open wide,
Everything will be prepared,
All you'll do is step inside."

"Here I am! I stand at the door and knock. If anyone
hears My voice and opens the door, I will come in
and eat with that person, and they with Me."
(Revelation 3:20)

Our Burdens Will Seem Dim

Life is full of discouragements
    And things that don't go our way,
Little obstacles meet our paths
    And discomforts reach our day.

But it we turn to God for help
    And cast our burdens on Him,
Our days will be bright again
    And our burdens will seem dim.

"Come to Me, all you who are weary and burdened, and I will give you rest. Take My yoke upon you and learn from Me, for I am gentle and humble in heart, and you will find rest for your souls. For My yoke is easy and My burden is light." (Matthew 11:28-30)

New Day

As the mist rises in the morning
And the sun brings in a new day,
Fill me Lord with Your blessing,
Keep me in Your will, this I pray.

Christ is the Only Way

Life on this earth is so short
And it is where we will decide
Where we spend eternity,
Will we in heaven abide?

Christ died on the cross for our sin
And He is the only way
That we can enter heaven
When we all die one day.

So, do not trust in yourselves
Or any good deed you may do
Nor any amount of money
Can ever help save you.

"For it is by grace you have been saved, through
faith - and this is not from yourselves, it is the gift
of God - not by works, so that no one can boast."
(Ephesians 2:8,9)

At Calvary

As leaves falling in the breeze
And softly hit the ground,
When my life on earth is over
My soul is heaven bound.

Not because I've been good,
But my life in Christ I place
Who died for me on Calvary,
And saved me by His grace.

God speaks to us through His Bible and through nature. Being out in nature is awesome and relaxing. The Bible speaks about how God created the heavens and earth, and He created both for us to enjoy. We can learn about God and His power through nature.

God also gave us the Bible so that we can learn about Him and His will for our lives. It speaks about how we are all sinners, and we are separated from God by our sin. Before the creation of the world, God planned a way to restore fellowship that was broken because of Adam and Eve's sin.

Jesus came to earth to die on the cross for all our sins. Salvation is trusting in the payment that Christ made on the cross in our place. When we trust Christ as our Savior, as a free gift, we can spend eternity with Him.

Salvation is not what we do, but what Jesus did for us. You can know you have eternal life because God is giving it to you when you put your faith in Jesus, because He died on the cross for all sin.

"I write these things to you who believe in the name of the Son of God so that you may know that you have eternal life." (1 John 5:13)

About the Author

Sandy Bohon is a Licensed Mental Health Counselor practicing in central Florida. She received her Bachelor's degree from Florida Bible College and a Master of Counseling degree from Liberty University. In her spare time, Sandy enjoys spending time with her family, going to the beach and gardening.

Other books by Sandy Bohon available on Amazon:

~ Joy in Overcoming Depression Through God's Word
~ JOY in Knowing Jesus Through God's Word
~ Poetry and Devotions for the Soul
~ Poetry and Devotions for the Soul for Youth
~ God's World Nature Poems
~ God's World Family Poems and Prayers
~ God's World Poetry for Teens

For more information please contact me:
  sandybohonlmhc@gmail.com
And join my mailing list at
  www.sandybohonlmhc.com

If you enjoyed this book please leave a a review on Amazon. Thanks!

Made in the USA
Monee, IL
01 February 2025

11413547R00044